Advent

Mike Logue

AOS Publishing, 2025

Copyright © 2025

Mike Logue

All rights reserved under International and
Pan-American copyright conventions

ISBN: 978-1-83432-025-0

Cover Design: Meredith Lindsay

Visit AOS Publishing's website:
www.aospublishing.com

Mike Logue is a Scot, retired and living in England. He holds an MA in Literature and Culture from the University of Salford. In addition to writing poetry, he is a researcher of the life and times of the Irish novelist Patrick MacGill, known as the 'Navvy Poet'.

Acknowledgments

Some of these poems have been previously published in anthologies, magazines, and online sites, including Poetry Scotland, The Open Mouse, Driech, Buzzin' Bards, Bards across the Pond, and Glasgow City of Poets.

Contents

Advent 1
Cross Quarter 2
Drift 3
Spring is suffering 4
Gleann nan Tri 5
Hard Ground 6
Remembrance 7
How would I know? 8
Knife in the wind 9
Biscay 10
Autumn into winter 11
Fading 12
Raasay 13
Heavy days, ... 14
Moor Top 15
River Inbhir 16
Sunt Kelda 17
The Baths 19
Under-wintering 20
Echo 21
Dazed 22
Expectations 23
Disturbing Context 24
Rosa December 25
Thaw 26
Night Drive 27

Sound of Water	28
What's in a name?	29
Portrait	31
River: Synecdoche	32
It crossed my mind	33
Still Life	34
Pastoral winter	36
Impair	37
Outburst	38
Above the beach	39
Dust	40
Fragments	41
Dreaming Again	42
As time is not necessarily linear,	43
Cotoneaster in flower	44
Words are watercolour	45
When you hear	46
Stained by run-off	47
Though we did not meet,	48
Cul-de-Sac conversation:	49
Festive/Autumn Colour	50

Advent

In the sullen days
of a temperate winter,

Dowdy green struggles,
bedraggled, among
the spare stalks....

Calendar says, the year is past!

Season says quietly, green has begun,
but not yet flowering.

Calendar says, new year to come!

Calendar says, new resolve
      — Be better than the last!

Season says quietly, you have no idea...
      — It will be what it will be.

Cross Quarter

Winter haze,
Candlemas days—

The chill of a frost,
sweating

Lenten days as
preparation

to be worthy of
the season coming

Demeter—
       waiting

Persephone—
       still slumming

Drift

Soft the snow
Light as an idea
Layer upon layer,
Until you are
Gripped

No beating of rain,
Leaking through seams
Into pockets and ears

No rattling and
thrashing of hail,
being browbeaten
into shelter.

Snow is seductive; it
holds you in a spell
as it draws your
warmth: it takes
you from yourself

Spring is suffering

Here but not,
Then here again;
The signs are thin

Blossom on the
Apple trees:
half there,
incomplete

ducklings on the canal
dash to and fro,
swept along in a breeze

the sun is afraid to show,
mugged by chilling air:
a fraudulent offer
of warmth

Washing lines, however,
are out of hibernation,

Waiting for the
swifts and swallows

Gleann nan Tri

Three waters meet,
mingle, and take
to their heels
—off down the glen.

Three sisters hunker
under the ridge,
feet in the waters.
No dreaming of Moscow

Three friends laze
as a lochan,
joined by the waters
—take to a river.

Course past Clachaig and
Carnoch to dissolve in
the salt of the Leven.

Hard Ground

Winter sun,
gorged on frost

grass shatters—frozen

Hard Ground
no give

What cannot bend is broken

Frost hangs
curtains all

Hard Air
rimes the senses

Remembrance

The moor under a blanket
of sodden snow—

Blowing horizontally—

Sticking to mountains
like a wet tee-shirt.

Pools and lochans blank,
Black water swallowing the light
with a malevolent glare

Desolate day—in the now

Souls driven from their hearths
to be lost in that winter past.

Desolate day—it was then;

Mists curtain the herdsmen
of the glen,

Shepherding the souls still

How would I know?

If I forgot you,
A nagging space
of shadowing,
sense of incomplete
sense of missing
something better—
feeling of something lesser.
A want to find,
Drawn to be somewhere
Not now knowing why

I would know the space,
The shape of empty
That led me
Before you

Knife in the wind

Drab days troupe
across the month,
sheepish heads down

February faces, scowling
in the grey light

are fists closed hard
against the knife
in the wind

Biscay

Winter skies greyed and
splashed with squalls of light;

Frayed curtains reflected
in the mirror of a pallid sea;

Windless waves sigh
and heave onto a shore.

Seasonal towns are out of season

Spare of life

Wrapped in resilience,

Waiting

Autumn into winter

The façade of summer
has fallen,

Decorum has been
dissolved in a season

—there is no disguise
on the land.

Hill and gully are etched
in the contours

—the climate is hard
on the land.

Soils are sodden,
grasses are drained

—the season expressed
on the land.

Hedgerows ripped
by flails

—there is no pretence
on the land.

Fading

The birch shines in
greying light,

Rustles and dazzles
in the gusts.

Leaves detach and
dance away

and decorate the decay.

Fallen leaves gather
      — my memories fading

Fallen leaves gather
      — my regrets unrepaired

Raasay

Hard days have come
to the girls of The Leac;

their garb is browned
and yellowed.

Now shed spring
and summer
as carpets of colour.

Dulled in their senses,
pale boled, they wait

To greet the
sleets and hails
of winter gales

Heavy days,

the view is thick

—air hazed with heat.

Hedgerows are overblown,
verges bloused and seedy

—unfreshed by rain

Biscuit / golden panels
of grain and stubble

—drape the contours

Balers are busy,
pastel packets

- litter the parks

A parade of limes
line the road: pollarded

—erase the shade

Tarmac

—summer scent

Moor Top

A wind scours grasses
leeched of colour,
limp, pallid straws
exhausted by winter,
with leavings of snow
etched in the hollows.

the hillsides lie bare,
pleading for succour,
begging the alms
of warmth in the weather
to bring up the grasses
that will clothe them for summer—

a wind scours hillsides
starved for a spring

River Inbhir

Amber/Black liquid moving down,
patiently waiting behind the weirs,

languidly gliding 'round banks and bends
to a point where the tranquility ends,

Now bundling and pushing 'round rocks,
roaring and foaming into pools

Black and Tan waters with a head of cream
—you know the brew.

Peat malted, Assynt water, mashed over
our oldest stones

Inbhir: river: seeking Loch

Sunt Kelda

No one remains
to drink at the well

—Your people are removed

From beginnings of beginnings,
you sheltered some few;
the settings are empty of life
they once grew

Isolated,
your people were sound,
their world you sealed,
with cliffs you bound

Isolation withered,
each landing a toll;
disease and religion
took body and soul

Ages moved on,
distances shrivelled,

no longer
—The edge of the world

The birds have it all,
lose no eggs to the climbers;
they are fodder for cameras
and tourist admirers

Dun still shelters,
Conachair still rises;

the stacks still sit
in the sea

—And your people are removed

The Baths

Beacon by Justice Mill
draws the wanderer

—From the wine dark Dee,

Siren panels, framing
a Rose-Coloured Dawn

 —Promising the day

Hard by Hardgate,
Lovely Young Dawn

—Held in a Bon Accord

For those who voyage,
to Albyn and beyond

Under-wintering

Frost on the slates:

First ice is here

Hydrangea is shocked,
Acers shiver in fear

Red and yellow
Are let go,

are fallen to
drab.

The dank of
solstice days
follows the
season of colour

Little growing,
at least
not showing,
through the
autumn debris

into shadow-time;

the submerged season
of
under-wintering

Echo

Part of me is an echo
sounding from a distance,
a shadow of the native,
the remains of an existence

holding an allegiance
to a fading reminiscence.

Part of me is an echo
calling on remembrance,
of news and sport and weather,
call centre discussions

refreshed by native accents
and email conversations.

Part of me is an echo
with native mores outdated,
blowing on the embers
but really...
        —disconnected

Dazed

You have such a beauty

I cannot define.

Words flee my pen;

my page has no line.

Description is hollow,

language has left.

You have such a beauty—

It has me bereft.

Expectations

I will die in a foreign land,
As it should be, perhaps?

Struggling with change,
Unlearning what has been learned
[or forgotten]

Amid half-understood
conventions,
with contemporaries
and icons no longer there,
        Any comfort zone is gone.

It comes slowly, though;
isolation,
It comes: loss of confidence
in movement,
in excursion.

it comes: loss of independence
and it comes: reliance on others
with age...

I will die in a foreign land,
As it should be—most likely!

Disturbing Context

Text in a landscape,
someone said

The thought of it
disturbed me

Out of context for me,
beyond my framework
of what I need
in a landscape

Spare expanses of contour,
colour, and texture, no place for text;
conversations are internal,
absorbing the images,
senses bare to weather

Me, a figure in a landscape—

Text in my landscape
would disturb,
would need analysis,
would need attention,
would need interpretation.

Is that the purpose
of text in a landscape?
to intrude a thought,
to foist an idea,
to infest a mind—
to disturb a body's context

Rosa December

Lean in stature, solitary blooms
conspicuous in the desert
that once was foliage

one pale with an edge of rose;
one rose with an edge of pale

A final gesture as the
season moves across
the solstice.

Break your gaze—
they are dissolved

Thaw

The thaw is bleak,
light is matt flat

Images leeched of colour
blink to be uncovered;

the shadow of snow remains
in the light not there

Night Drive

In the light,
Colour is strewn as debris:
Heather dank,
Bracken rust,
Deergrass red,
       sometime yellow

The days of a season dying

By the verges;
in the edges of the
Headlights, shapes appear,
Shades drift by—
      —Silent souls

A head is turned, lifts a gaze,
Eyes afire—
Did I know you?
      Can you tell me who I used to be?

Sound of Water

The sound of water comes

Ripples across a pond
          —through the air

Lapping at the imagination;
—a sound of what?
            —from where?
a jumper,
            maybe?

At a bridge,
            definitely
a jumper!

The sound of water comes,

the wash of an eddy
          —stilling a mind

What's in a name?

[for James Hawkins of Rhue]

Were you summoned by the *Spot?*
—To the north?
What was the word that was writ?

That set you out on mountain'd seas,
With crests of schist and grit

Forms you captured by eye and hand
—Treasure of the heart and the mind
—Treasure in colour on the canvas

And should the Old Sea Cook
put into your haven

What would be the form?

"Come away Hawkins," he would say
"Come and have a yarn,"

You would tell your news, of
what has been built
between hill and shore;

And more, of the
treasures of your soul
charting their being from
then until now,

and how
they have taken to voyages of their own

"Ah," would say Silver, "it were fortunate that they had Hawkins by them."

Portrait

A phrase, earworm image
of place or colour,
ticks away in my mind.

Sporadic at best.
not driven to pen,
refusing to be on paper
until formed.

Summer gives soft,
blousy shapes
and decorum

Winter in my mind
gives the edge,
the drama in landscape,
phrases of colour,
dark, bare,
sparse landforms

Stark is home—

Winter without sun—
        rain: rain: rain

River: Synecdoche

The line was,
"*The river is still the same*"
a throwaway, a
recall of place, of
encounter with
an acquaintance.

In view is a fraction of
a current existence, no
certain knowledge of
what has preceded, no
view of what might
be once passed.

Constant changes
on and under a surface,
forces we do not see or
know of, are acting

Knowing only what is
presented at that time
and place.

A river is never *still the same,*

As we all are

It crossed my mind

As the pigeon crossed the view,
Speeding in a straight line:
North to south

Not loitering in the garden,
ungainly and glowering at
the bird feeder,

This pigeon had a
purpose in mind,

but what?

Might not be understandable—
If not a pigeon

Might only be from A to B,

But then why B?

Would it help to know?

Still Life

The image was there
      to be taken;

Then it was gone,
      dissolved
        to another form.

Layers of green,
      gold-fingered,
fringed in the red
      of new growth.

Star jumps of foliage,
      strata sprawling,
dancing sunlit
      In the breeze.

Changeling

The image was
      again
star jumps
    transmuted to
      arcs and slopes,

hard edges
      softened,
colours now
      sparkling
        green and gold,

fronds etched
      in red

            acer under the rain—
still life

Pastoral winter

Veils are cast,
Seasons have danced

Fields and hollows
Once hidden
Are undone

The secret spaces
Of landscape are
 scraped clean
Of decorum

Buildings and sheds
Hunker and huddle,
Embarrassed,
Unable to flee

Stubbornly waiting
For the music;

For the dance
To begin

Impair

    Croissants bought in pairs,
a Sunday breakfast

    two apiece, but I need only one

      Do I say? "Buy only three"

    Would it break the symmetry?

    Would it tip the balance?

To be not matched

Outburst

The dark of distant rain
smothers the day,
rinses summer greens
in swathes of grey.

no gentle mists
no 'soft day' this

fierce waters hounding/
slashing/pounding:

blooms beheaded,
roses shredded,
flora drowning:

...and
...it passes—
tirade over,
rage exhausted...

...light limps
back
into
the day

Above the beach

There was a moment; above the beach
I found something I had lost,
or perhaps forgotten

you turned in the sun
and the light caught in your eye,

and revelation,
perhaps remembrance,
crystal bright, hazel green,
shone for a moment and
surprised my complacence

where had they been,
prisms so clear

where had I been looking,
and you always near,

and now I wait
for the situation
where there is light
that might be
to let your eyes
shine green

Dust

Don't bury me;
Make me dust;
Reduce me to ashes;

Spread me in a wind,
Who knows where.

I won't know the dead
are not aware—

It's for the living to
anchor the memory
held in their care

Fragments

What a clumsy tool is memory,
fragments of a story, misremembered
of place and time
by those who were there.

Fragments are the ties we share,
mostly out of place and out of time,
which is when is hard to tell

Friendship is built upon such fragments, a mosaic
to be the whole,
       the constant,
              the background buzz,
                      the scenery of life and self.
It is in the mind, just a thought away, to hold the spell

Dreaming Again

I am dreaming again;
No, not quite right—
I am remembering that I dream

In the past, no memory
of dreams, yet
they were surely there

Now I know I am dreaming
when I am in a dream

no sense of logic,
only of accepting it.

no sense of the matter,
attempting to resolve,

Marking a shift in life

I cannot follow my dreams
      —too chaotic and unclear

but I will watch as I sleep

As time is not necessarily linear,

so the past is not necessarily
a trail of dusty footprints
of paths taken or not.

Our past is what makes us
[present tense, not past]
It is bundled up
beneath us,
a foundation, a base to
reach beyond ourselves

Our past is in the future;
It is yet to be

Cotoneaster in flower

hums and buzzes like
a motorway

A dodgem track of bees
ducking and diving
for the pollen

Singing the early summer

Fruit is forming,
pollen is finishing,
bees are dispersing—

Summer is elsewhere

Words are watercolour

splashed on a page,
shades of meaning
with ambiguous grace

My mind does not hold fast;
words wash and eddy between
intention and form

My mind is a washing machine;
needs a spin to put
words on a line

When you hear

Sparrows bickering
in a hedge—

Geese mumbling
in flight—

Magpies' sarcastic
bravura—

Tits chattering as
they forage—

Goldfinches wittering
on a wire—

Niños buzzing,
queued for
Zarzuela—

What do you know?

Stained by run-off

after rain

taking its cue from
the season's decay,
canal water is the
colour of clay

carrying birch leaves
scarlet and gold
corralled by the breeze

colour carpet;
yellow
to red
on the path

sodden,
downtrodden

in the early light

puddles
like glass,
stepping away

Though we did not meet,

the course of your star
was followed.

Each wax and wane
was attended until
your final fade.

If we are but nothing,
held only in the memory
of others, then

you are here,
held in us all,
most strongly by those
who held you dear.

you will be—
as long as memory remains,

Electra Remembered

Cul-de-Sac conversation:

What's new?
Nothing much
What was lunch?
>Something,
>Not much.
>No taste.

Fraises for taste, chain-smoked, devoured.

Café for taste, bolted.

Routine—morning:
>Daily bread and other domestic needs

Routine—afternoon:
Café and fraises

Insipid days,
Impatient for release

Festive/Autumn Colour

Stubble blond
grey

Birch yellow
grey

Bracken rust
grey

Furrow black
grey

Holly green
grey

Berry red
grey

Grey
grey

www.ingramcontent.com/pod-product-compliance
Lightning Source LLC
LaVergne TN
LVHW012037060526
838201LV00061B/4649